Maxine
the
Meanie

L.D. ETHERLY
CHASE VELARDE

Maxine The Meanie

L.D. Etherly Copyright Text © 2011-2013

Chase Velarde Copyright Illustration © 2013

All Rights Reserved.

Summary: Rhyming book about a reformed bully named Maxine

ISBN-13: 978-0983387756 (InKspil Publishing)

ISBN-10: 0983387753

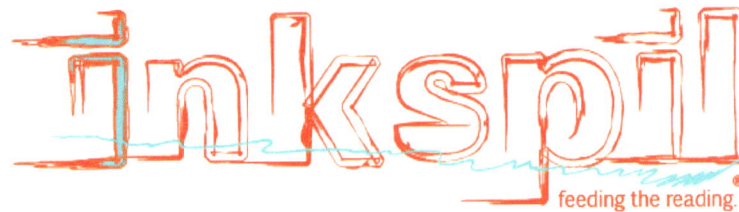

inkspil
feeding the reading.®

www.InKspil.com
Chicago, Illinois

Printed in the United States of America

Dedicated to children everywhere,
be inspired!

L. D. Ethelry

Maxine the Meanie was Known all over town.
The rumors said she wore a permanent frown.

Maxine was rude
and never had anything nice to say.

When she would speak to the other children, they'd cry and run away.

Maxine was the worst when she had nothing to do.

She would throw rocks at windows or hide other kid's shoes.

Maxine would laugh when she made someone cry.
She enjoyed being mean, but she didn't Know why.

One morning, she went outside and

on her door, there was a letter;

"Dear Maxine,

why do you put others down to make yourself feel better? Did you know that you don't HAVE to be so terribly mean? You can be a nice person, if you just raised your self esteem!"

This letter bugged and bothered Maxine all day.

Finally she realized,
she didn't know how to be any other way.

Maxine felt wretched
and simply horrible inside.

She wanted to talk it out,

but had no one in whom she could confide.

Maxine had so many emotions that she needed to express.

So, she grabbed a pen and paper and let out her stress!

The more she drew the less she wanted to shout.

Soon all of her negative emotions had been let out.

Maxine decided that she didn't want to put her pen down.

She'd rather draw pictures of the people in her town.

Maxine drew, and drew,

then drew some more,

Drawing made her happy

and let her spirit soar.

Now she could be Kind
while giving her drawings away.
Everyone noticed the big difference
and gave Maxine a "Hooray!"

Maxine the Meanie
had created a new rapport,
because Maxine the Meanie
was a meanie no more!

Vocabulary Definition Depot

Emotions
The mood or feelings of a person.

Permanent
Something that lasts for a very long time or forever.

Rapport
A peaceful relationship with others.

Self Esteem
Being happy with yourself.

Wretched
Unhappy or very sad.

What should you do if you are being bullied?

Clearly express yourself and tell the bully to "Stop!"

Tell an ADULT you trust.

Ask your friends for help.

Share your story with others.

What should you do if you see someone being bullied?

Find a responsible adult and tell them what you saw.

Listen and encourage the person who has been bullied.

Share your story with others.

What should you do if you are a bully?

Listen to someone who says "Stop!"

Change your behavior and learn to respect others.

Ask for help.

Share your story with others.

L. D. Etherly

Author

L. D. Etherly was and born and raised in Chicago, Illinois where she currently lives with her husband and two adorable daughters.

Etherly loves to write creative and enriching stories for children of all ages. Her inspiration is found in daily parental experiences and her ability to captivate imagination and wonderment is the reason her titles are so widely sought after.

Her stories include themes of love, acceptance and conflict resolution and are perfect teaching tools for home, school and children activity centers.

L. D. Etherly's titles include: *When I Fall Asleep*, *Winter Arrives This Summer*, *Baxter The Bully* and *Maxine The Meanie,* all of which are available through Inkspil Publishing.

Chase Velarde

Chase Velarde was born in Forest Grove, Oregon in the spring of 1988. He started drawing at the age of three, and won his first award in kindergarten.

Illustrator

At the tender age of six, he shrewdly turned a homemade lemonade-stand into an art-stand which showcased his first gallery. The art stand was wildly popular with his parents, and he sensed a future in the field, so, intrepidly, he pushed on.

Growing up in the tiny town of Yamhill, Oregon, Chase found inspiration in the natural world and the curious ways of living things. His love of discovery, along with his love of cartoons, comics, and books drove him to pursue a future in illustration, and in 2007 he moved to Portland to attend the Pacific Northwest College of Art. Soon after he began working as a freelance artist and has been living out his dream as an illustrator since.

Be kind .

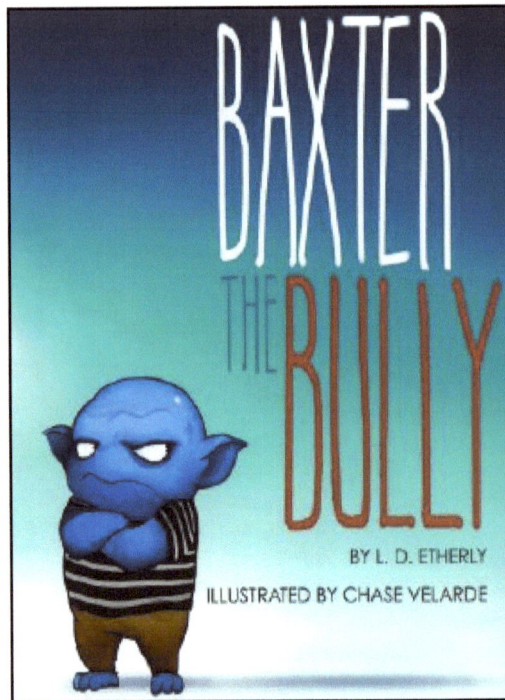

www.ingramcontent.com/pod-product-compliance
Lightning Source LLC
Chambersburg PA
CBHW042125040426
42450CB00002B/75